WORKBOOK

For

Help Me, I'm Stuck

Six Proven Methods to Shift Your Mindset From Self-Sabotage to Self-Improvement (The Help Me Series)

An Interactive Guide to Vaughn Carter's Book

Flawless Prints

Companion Workbook for [Help Me, I'm Stuck]

Copyright © 2023 by [Flawless Prints]

All rights reserved. No part of this workbook may be reproduced, distributed, or transmitted in any form or by any means, including photocopying, recording, or other electronic or mechanical methods, without the prior written permission of the publisher, except in the case of brief quotations embodied in critical reviews and certain other noncommercial uses permitted by copyright law.

This companion workbook is designed to be used in conjunction with the original book, [Help Me, I'm Stuck=]," authored by [Vaughn Carter]. It is intended to enhance the reader's understanding of the concepts presented in the original book and provide a structured framework for exercises, activities, and reflection.

Please note that this workbook is not a standalone publication and is not intended to replace the original book. It is recommended that readers possess a copy of the original book to fully benefit from the content provided in this workbook.

Table of Contents

How to Use this Workbook 4

Summary 8

A Focused Mind Leaves the Stuck Behind 12

    Key Takeaways 12

    Prompts for Self-Reflection 14

The Power of Positive Thinking 24

    Key Takeaways 24

    Prompts for Self-Reflection 25

Gratitude 36

    Key Takeaways 36

    Prompts for Self-Reflection 38

Foods and Fitness for Positive Thinking 48

    Key Takeaways 48

    Prompts for Self-Reflection 51

How to Eliminate Negative Thoughts 62

    Key Takeaways 62

    Prompts for Self-Reflection 65

Empathy 76

    Key Takeaways 76

    Prompts for Self-Reflection 78

Self-Evaluation Prompts..88

How to Use this Workbook

Welcome to this companion workbook for the book [Help Me, I'm Stuck]. This workbook is designed to help you deepe your understanding of the key concepts and principles presented in the book and apply them to your own life.

Getting Started

Before you begin working through the workbook, it is recommended that you read the original book [Help Me, I'm Stuck] to gain a comprehensive understanding of the content. Once you have completed the book, you can start using this workbook to further explore the material and personalize your learning experience.

Structure of the Workbook

This workbook is organized into chapters that correspond to the chapters in the original book. Each chapter includes the following sections:

Key Takeaways: This section summarizes the main points and insights from the corresponding chapter in the book.

Self-Reflection Prompts: This section provides a series of questions to guide your reflection on the chapter's content and your personal experiences related to the topic.

How to Use the Workbook

Here are some suggestions for using this workbook effectively:

Read the Key Takeaways: Before delving into the self-reflection prompts, take some time to review the Key Takeaways for the chapter. This will refresh your memory of the main concepts and prepare you for deeper reflection.

Engage with the Self-Reflection Prompts: Take the time to thoughtfully answer each of the self-reflection prompts. Write down your responses or reflect on them quietly. The prompts are designed to encourage introspection and personal application of the chapter's content.

Personalize Your Learning: Use the self-reflection prompts as a springboard for further exploration of the chapter's topics. Consider applying the concepts to your own life, drawing from personal experiences and observations.

Seek Support: If you find yourself struggling with any of the self-reflection prompts or feel overwhelmed by the material, don't hesitate to reach out to a trusted friend, family member, or mental health professional for support.

Self-Evaluation Prompts

At the end of the workbook, you will find a section titled "Self-Evaluation Prompts." These prompts are designed to help you assess your overall progress and identify areas for continued growth. Take some time to reflect on these prompts and consider how you can continue to integrate the insights and principles from the workbook into your life.

Additional Tips

Here are some additional tips for getting the most out of this workbook:

Set aside dedicated time each week to work through the workbook.

Find a quiet and distraction-free environment to focus on your reflections.

Use a notebook or journal to record your reflections and insights.

Review your reflections periodically to track your progress and identify areas for further exploration.

Remember, this workbook is a tool to guide your personal growth and self-discovery. Use it at your own pace, and don't hesitate to revisit the material as needed.

SUMMARY

"Help Me, I'm Stuck: Six Proven Methods to Shift Your Mindset From Self-Sabotage to Self-Improvement," by Vaughn Carter, is a self-help book that walks readers through a practical and effective strategy for overcoming emotions of stagnation and attaining personal progress. Carter recognizes self-sabotage as a major impediment to growth, and he offers six critical tactics for breaking free from these self-limiting behaviors and embracing self-improvement.

Determine Your Self-Sabotage Strategies: Recognizing the prevalence of self-sabotage in your life is the first step in overcoming it. Carter invites readers to examine their actions and uncover reoccurring patterns that impede their advancement. Procrastination, negative self-talk, and succumbing to distractions are all examples of this.

Understand the Root Causes: Once self-sabotage patterns have been discovered, it is critical to investigate their root causes. Carter recommends looking at prior events, belief systems, and emotional triggers that may have contributed to these actions. Understanding the underlying issues enables individuals to successfully address them.

Negative Self-Talk: Negative self-talk is a common kind of self-sabotage that undermines confidence and drive. Carter highlights the significance of questioning the veracity of negative beliefs and replacing them with more positive and uplifting affirmations.

Embrace Positive Thinking: It is critical to cultivate a positive mentality in order to break away from self-sabotage. Carter urges readers to focus on their abilities, be proud of their successes, and have a positive attitude. This alteration in viewpoint has the potential to greatly improve motivation and resilience.

Setting unreasonable objectives can lead to disappointment and setbacks, which can encourage self-sabotage. Carter argues for SMART objectives, which are Specific, Measurable, Achievable, Relevant, and Time-bound. These well-defined goals give a clear path forward and lessen the possibility of feeling overwhelmed.

Seek Help and Guidance: Overcoming self-sabotage frequently necessitates the assistance of others. Carter suggests that readers seek advice from reliable friends, family members, therapists, or mentors. These people may offer significant insights, encouragement, and accountability while on the path to self-improvement.

Carter's book offers a thorough and practical foundation for overcoming self-sabotage and growing personally. Individuals may create a positive mentality, establish realistic objectives, and embrace self-improvement by detecting self-sabotage behaviors, understanding their core causes, and applying the solutions mentioned. "Help Me, I'm Stuck" is a motivating handbook for those looking to change their life and attain their greatest potential.

A Focused Mind Leaves the Stuck Behind

Key Takeaways

Overcoming self-sabotage requires a concentrated mind.

You can do the following with a concentrated mind:

Establish clear objectives and priorities. When you're focused, you're better able to establish your goals and devise a strategy to attain them.

Distractions should be avoided. When you're focused, you're less likely to get distracted by social media, email, or other distractions.

Maintain your motivation. When you're focused, you're more likely to stick to your goals and persist in the face of adversity.

Carter presents various ways for building a concentrated mind in the chapter, including:

Mindfulness is being practiced. The discipline of paying attention to the present moment without judgment is known as mindfulness. This can assist you in becoming more aware of your thoughts and feelings, as well as letting go of distractions.

Making time for concentrated work. Schedule time each day to focus solely on your most essential goals.

Dividing enormous work into smaller ones. Large chores can be daunting, leading to procrastination. By breaking things down into smaller, more manageable stages, they might appear less intimidating and more doable.

Rewarding yourself for your accomplishments. Take some time to celebrate your successes as you work toward your goals. This will assist you in remaining motivated and going forward.

You may overcome self-sabotage and achieve your goals by cultivating a concentrated mind.

Prompts for Self-Reflection

How do you tell whether your mind is focused?

What are some of your sources of distraction?

Have you tried mindfulness meditation before? If so, how did you find it?

_____
_____
_____
_____
_____
_____
_____
_____
_____
_____
_____
_____
_____
_____
_____
_____
_____
_____
_____
_____
_____
_____

What are some more ways you may incorporate mindfulness into your daily life?

How many hours do you spend each day on concentrated work?

What are some of the difficulties you encounter while attempting to devote time to concentrated work?

When was the last time you put off doing something?

What factors do you believe contribute to major jobs becoming overwhelming?

What are some of the ways you thank yourself for your achievements?

How can rewarding oneself assist you in remaining motivated?

THE POWER OF POSITIVE THINKING

Key Takeaways

Positive thought has the power to change our life. When we concentrate on the positive aspects of our lives, we are more likely to feel joyful, confident, and driven.

Our world is created by our ideas and beliefs. Our experiences are shaped by our beliefs about ourselves and the world around us. We create a more favorable world for ourselves when we nurture optimistic thinking.

We may learn to manage our emotions and ideas. We can all learn to focus on the good and let rid of negative ideas with practice.

Neglecting our difficulties is not the goal of positive thinking. It is a matter of admitting them and then deciding to concentrate on solutions.

Positive thinking is a talent that can be learned. The more we practice, the better we get.

We may fight self-sabotage and achieve our goals by adding positive thinking into our lives.

Prompts for Self-Reflection

When was the last time you felt the power of positive thinking?

How do you usually feel when you think positively?

What are some of your fundamental ideas about yourself and the world?

What effect do these beliefs have on your thoughts, feelings, and actions?

_____
_____
_____
_____
_____
_____
_____
_____
_____
_____
_____
_____
_____
_____
_____
_____
_____
_____
_____
_____
_____

What are some of your negative thought triggers?

What are some ways to manage your thoughts and emotions?

How do you usually cope with difficulties and setbacks?

What are some strategies for approaching difficulties with a good attitude?

What are some of the ways you've used positive thinking in your life?

What tools have you used to help you improve your positive thinking skills?

_____
_____
_____
_____
_____
_____
_____
_____
_____
_____
_____
_____
_____
_____
_____
_____
_____
_____
_____
_____
_____
_____

GRATITUDE

Key Takeaways

Gratitude is the ability to perceive the good in every circumstance, especially when things are difficult. We adjust our perspective and educate our minds to focus on the positive when we focus on the things we are grateful for. This has the potential to have a significant influence on our overall happiness and well-being.

Gratitude can assist us in overcoming self-sabotage. We are less prone to concentrate on our flaws or compare ourselves to others when we are appreciative for what we have. This can assist us in breaking away from negative thought patterns and moving on with our objectives.

There are several methods to express thanks. Some individuals keep a thankfulness diary, while others simply spend a few moments each day to reflect on their blessings. You may also thank them by telling them how much you value their presence in your life.

Gratitude is a strong tool that may assist us in leading happier, healthier, and more satisfying lives.

Additional Gratitude Practice Suggestions:

Begin small. Don't try to enumerate everything you're thankful for all at once. Begin by listing a few things you are grateful for each day.

Make your point. The more detailed you are about what you are glad for, the greater the impact of your appreciation.

Concentrate on the current moment. It is easy to become preoccupied with anxieties about the future or regrets about the past. However, it is critical to concentrate on the positive developments that are taking place right now.

Share your appreciation with others. Telling someone you appreciate them may make both of you happy.

Prompts for Self-Reflection

Can you think of a time when you felt the power of thankfulness, even under difficult circumstances? What effect did it have on your viewpoint and attitude to the situation?

_____
_____
_____
_____
_____
_____
_____
_____
_____
_____
_____
_____
_____
_____
_____
_____
_____

How do you usually feel after practicing gratitude? Does it cause you to shift your attitude from negativity to appreciation?

How can concentrating on flaws and comparing oneself to others lead to self-destructive behavior?

How can focusing on thankfulness help you break away from negative thought patterns and develop good self-esteem?=

Have you thought of maintaining a gratitude journal? If so, how have you found this practice to be?

What additional ways do you incorporate gratitude into your everyday life, such as thanking people or meditating on your blessings?

How has practicing thankfulness influenced your general happiness and well-being? Provide detailed instances.

What beneficial improvements in your relationships, perspective, and overall approach to life have you observed as a result of your appreciation practice?

What are your long-term objectives for cultivating thankfulness and its good influence in your life?

_____
_____
_____
_____
_____
_____
_____
_____
_____
_____
_____
_____
_____
_____
_____
_____
_____
_____

Foods and Fitness for Positive Thinking

Key Takeaways

Key Lesson 1: Your mood and energy levels are directly affected by what you consume.

When we eat nutritious meals, our bodies and minds perform optimally. We're feeling more enthusiastic, concentrated, and upbeat. In contrast, eating unhealthy meals might cause mood fluctuations, weariness, and difficulties concentrating.

Key Lesson 2: Physical and mental wellness require exercise.

Endorphins, which have mood-boosting properties, are released as a result of regular exercise. It also aids in the reduction of stress, anxiety, and sadness. Exercise can also help with sleep, which is vital for mood regulation and brain clarity.

A person running on a treadmill is seen.

Key Lesson 3: Making healthy lifestyle choices might be challenging, but it is worthwhile in the long term.

Making long-term adjustments to your food and exercise habits requires time and work. The advantages to your physical and emotional wellbeing, on the other hand, are enormous. You are more likely to feel good about yourself emotionally if you feel good about yourself physically.

Key Lesson 4: There are several tools available to assist you in making healthy lifestyle adjustments.

There are several books, websites, and applications available to help you with knowledge and assistance. You can also get tailored counsel from your doctor or a trained dietician.

Key Lesson 5: Don't be hesitant to try new things to see what works best for you.

Because everyone is unique, there is no one-size-fits-all strategy to healthy living. Find a diet and fitness regimen that you love and that works with your schedule.

Suggestions for Making Healthy Changes:

Set attainable objectives. Don't try to change your entire way of life all at once. Begin with minor modifications that you can maintain.

Choose an activity that you enjoy. Don't force yourself to run if you don't enjoy it. Swimming, dancing, and sports are all excellent ways to get some exercise.

Make healthy options more accessible. Keep healthful foods on hand and arrange time for exercise.

Don't be hesitant to seek assistance. For individualized advice, see your doctor or a qualified dietician.

Prompts for Self-Reflection

How do you usually feel after a nutritious meal? How do you feel after eating junk food?

Have you observed any correlations between your eating habits and your mood or energy levels?

What are your current workout routines? How frequently do you participate in physical activity?

Have you seen any differences in your mood, energy, or stress levels after beginning or increasing your exercise routine?

_____
_____
_____
_____
_____
_____
_____
_____
_____
_____
_____
_____
_____
_____
_____
_____
_____
_____
_____
_____
_____

What obstacles have you encountered in the past while attempting to make healthy changes?

_____
_____
_____
_____
_____
_____
_____
_____
_____
_____
_____
_____
_____
_____
_____
_____
_____
_____
_____

What are some techniques you might employ to overcome these obstacles and keep on track with your objectives?

What resources have been useful to you in your path to a healthy lifestyle?

Are there any specific resources you'd want to look into further?

What are some healthy behaviors you've successfully implemented in your life?

What are some of the difficulties you've had in establishing new healthy habits?

How to Eliminate Negative Thoughts

Key Takeaways

Lesson 1: Recognize Your Negative Thought Patterns

The first step in getting rid of negative ideas is being aware of them. Pay attention to your thoughts throughout the day, and pay attention to when you begin to think negatively. You may begin to fight your negative thinking patterns after you've identified them.

Key Lesson 2: Question the Veracity of Your Negative Thoughts

Not every negative notion is correct. When you have a bad notion, consider if it is true. Is there proof to back up your claim, or is it simply a wild guess?

Key Lesson 3: Reframe Your Thoughts (Key Lesson 3)

After you have questioned the veracity of your negative thinking, you may rephrase it in a more positive manner. Instead of thinking, "I'm not good enough, " consider, "I am capable, and I can achieve anything I set my mind to. "

Key Lesson 4: Practice Mindfulness

The discipline of paying attention to the present moment without judgment is known as mindfulness. This can assist you in being more aware of your thoughts and feelings, as well as in letting go of unpleasant thoughts.

Key Lesson 5: Replace Negative Thoughts with Positive Thoughts

It is critical to replace negative thoughts with positive ones as they arise. This might be challenging at first, but it becomes simpler with experience.

How to Get Rid of Negative Thoughts

Maintain a thinking journal. This might assist you in identifying negative thinking patterns.

Consult a therapist. A therapist can assist you in developing skills for combating negative thoughts.

Use positive self-talk. This might assist you in combating negative thinking.

Surround yourself with individuals who are upbeat. The individuals you spend your time with have a tremendous influence on your views.

Take physical care of oneself. Eating well, getting enough sleep, and exercising on a regular basis can all help to boost your mood and make it easier to deal with unpleasant thoughts.

Remember that getting rid of negative ideas requires time and effort. Don't give up and be patient with yourself. You may learn to regulate your thoughts and develop a more optimistic mentality with practice.

Prompts for Self-Reflection

What are some particular instances or triggers that cause you to have negative thoughts?

_____
_____
_____
_____
_____
_____
_____
_____
_____
_____
_____
_____
_____
_____
_____
_____
_____
_____
_____
_____
_____

How can you know when you are talking to yourself negatively? Is there anything bodily or emotional that indicates this shift in thinking?

Have you ever discovered yourself thinking negatively without examining their validity?

What tactics can you use to question the underlying assumptions or ideas that are the source of your negative thoughts?

What are some alternate viewpoints or reframes to consider when confronted with a negative thought?

How can you change your attention away from self-criticism and toward self-compassion and encouragement?

Have you tried any mindfulness activities like meditation or breathing exercises? How has your experience been using these techniques?

_____
_____
_____
_____
_____
_____
_____
_____
_____
_____
_____
_____
_____
_____
_____
_____
_____
_____

How can you apply mindfulness into your everyday routine to increase your awareness of your thoughts and emotions?

_____
_____
_____
_____
_____
_____
_____
_____
_____
_____
_____
_____
_____
_____
_____
_____
_____
_____
_____
_____
_____
_____
_____

What methods have you used to replace negative ideas with good thoughts? How successful have these methods been?

How can you build a more positive outlook by surrounding yourself with good people and participating in uplifted activities?

Empathy

Key Takeaways

Key Lesson 1: The ability to comprehend and share the sentiments of others is defined as empathy. It is the capacity to put oneself in the shoes of another person and experience the world through their eyes.

Key Lesson 2: Empathy is a critical quality for developing meaningful connections. It enables us to interact with others on a more personal level, fostering trust and rapport.

Key Lesson 3: Empathy may also aid in the resolution of difficulties and disputes. We are more likely to develop a solution that works for everyone if we can grasp the other person's point of view.

Key Lesson 4: It is not always simple to develop empathy. To genuinely appreciate someone else's experience, we must set aside our preconceptions and judgments.

However, there are several things we can do to develop our empathy abilities. We may listen actively, attempt to see things from other people's points of view, and be prepared to suspend our judgment.

How to Improve Your Empathy Skills

Take note of nonverbal clues. Facial expressions, body language, and tone of voice are all examples of nonverbal communication.

Pose inquiries. This is an excellent approach to learn more about someone else's experience.

Pay attention. Don't let your thoughts or your phone distract you.

Validate the sentiments of the other person. This does not need you to agree with them, but it does require you to acknowledge their sentiments.

Avoid passing judgment. This simply serves to make the other person defensive and shut down.

Remember that empathy is a talent that must be developed over time. However, it is a talent worth honing. We may develop better connections, handle issues more efficiently, and have a more happy life when we can connect with others on a deeper level.

Prompts for Self-Reflection

In what instances have you found yourself naturally relating on a sympathetic level with others?

What influence has empathy had on your capacity to form meaningful connections and promote trust?

How has empathy helped you to enhance your existing relationships and make new ones?

What role has empathy had in settling disagreements or confrontations with others?

Consider a time when empathy enabled you to tackle a challenge or disagreement in a more constructive and understanding manner.

_____
_____
_____
_____
_____
_____
_____
_____
_____
_____
_____
_____
_____
_____
_____
_____
_____
_____
_____
_____
_____

How has empathy helped you discover common ground and cooperate with others to come up with mutually beneficial solutions?

What personal obstacles or prejudices have you experienced when attempting to improve your empathy skills?

How have you overcome these obstacles and developed a more open and empathetic attitude toward the experiences of others?

What particular strategies, such as active listening or focused questioning, have you implemented to improve your empathy?

How has being present and attentive in your dealings with others helped you connect with them on an empathic level?

Self-Evaluation Prompts

1. Consider your progress through this workbook. What were your significant takeaways or insights from the activities and prompts?

_____
_____
_____
_____
_____
_____
_____
_____
_____
_____
_____
_____
_____
_____
_____
_____
_____
_____
_____
_____

2. Determine the areas in which you have made substantial development or improvements. What particular changes or personal development have you noticed?

_____
_____
_____
_____
_____
_____
_____
_____
_____
_____
_____
_____
_____
_____
_____
_____
_____
_____
_____
_____

3. Recognize areas that still require attention or improvement. What specific aims or issues do you want to address in the future?

_____
_____
_____
_____
_____
_____
_____
_____
_____
_____
_____
_____
_____
_____
_____
_____
_____
_____

4. Evaluate your overall happiness with your participation in this workbook. What features did you find the most beneficial or useful?

_____
_____
_____
_____
_____
_____
_____
_____
_____
_____
_____
_____
_____
_____
_____
_____
_____

5. Assess the usefulness of the organization, content, and prompts in the workbook. What ideas do you have for improving its value to future users?

6. Consider your learning style and interests. What tactics or approaches did you find to be the most beneficial in putting the workbook's material into action?

_____
_____
_____
_____
_____
_____
_____
_____
_____
_____
_____
_____
_____
_____
_____
_____
_____
_____
_____
_____

7. Consider your readiness to continue adopting the workbook's concepts and techniques into your daily life. What concrete promises or acts do you intend to make?

_____
_____
_____
_____
_____
_____
_____
_____
_____
_____
_____
_____
_____
_____
_____
_____
_____
_____
_____
_____

8. Assess the workbook's influence on your self-awareness, comprehension, and personal progress. What effect has it had on your viewpoint and attitude to various elements of your life?

___

9. Evaluate your overall sense of achievement or fulfillment as a result of finishing this workbook. What thoughts or sentiments do you connect with your growth and accomplishments?

_____
_____
_____
_____
_____
_____
_____
_____
_____
_____
_____
_____
_____
_____
_____
_____
_____

10. Share any further thoughts, observations, or comments you have about the content, efficacy, or potential enhancements for future users of the workbook.

_____
_____
_____
_____
_____
_____
_____
_____
_____
_____
_____
_____
_____
_____
_____
_____
_____
_____
_____
_____

Made in the USA
Monee, IL
27 January 2025